THE KETO INSTANTPOT RECIPE BOOK

Easy to Make

Ketogenic Diet Recipes

Published in 2018 by
H&L Group

KETOSIS - WHAT IS IT?

Your body usually produces fuel to support regular system functions through a metabolic process known as glycolysis in which glucose (sugar) is broken down to be used as energy by the body's cells. When there is an insufficient supply of glucose from carbohydrates in the diet, a metabolic shift will occur in which the body's carbohydrate stores, known as glycogen, will become the body's primary fuel source. Once glycogen stores have been depleted (2-3 days), the liver begins producing ketone bodies. Ketone bodies are molecules that can be used as an alternative fuel source by cells and originate from fatty acids. Therefore, when the body is in ketosis, fat stores are mobilized to create energy to be used by the body's cells thus facilitating fat mass loss resulting in observable weight loss.

THE KETOGENIC DIET

With the prevalence of cardiovascular disease, type 2 diabetes, obesity and other chronic diseases on the rise, many diets and metabolic strategies have come to light and are being put to the test. One of those diets, with growing popularity, is the keto diet.

The keto diet is a low-carbohydrate, high-fat diet that shares similarities with the Atkins diet. However, unlike the Atkins Diet which works in phases, the keto diet does not which simplifies things. The carbohydrate restriction ranges from 50 grams per day down to 20 grams per day. Starting at the lower end of low-carbohydrate is known to expedite the metabolic switch to ketone bodies.

Anyone following a keto diet will agree that at first, you will feel sluggish. This is because the metabolic change from high-carb to low-carb depletes your body's 2-3 day carbohydrate stores known as glycogen. During this process, you will also lose water weight. Once you have exhausted your carbohydrate stores, ketosis (fat burning) will result. Following this metabolic switch, the sluggishness will dissipate.

The induction of ketosis is beneficial for multiple reasons. Firstly, when you eat carbohydrates your blood sugar rises, and as a result, your pancreas secretes insulin. Insulin functions as a storage hormone by opening the door to cells to allow the sugar to come rushing in to act as fuel and to also reduce blood sugars back to normal levels; if the cell is provided with excess energy (sugar), it will be stored as fat for later use. When this high blood sugar/insulin response mechanism doesn't work properly, it is known as type 2 diabetes. When dramatically reducing the amount of carbohydrates in the diet, the insulin response occurs to a much lower degree thus avoiding weight gain through this particular mechanism. Studies have reported reduced blood sugar levels as well as insulin levels in those who follow a keto diet which is beneficial for those at risk or for those who currently have type II diabetes.

Secondly, this diet facilitates weight loss. Considering you are no longer at risk of storing excess carbs as fat AND you are now using fat as a primary energy source, weight loss is inevitable. Fat mass is simply stored energy waiting to be used. When you induce ketosis, your body must use fat in order to make ketone bodies to fuel your system and your brain. Thirdly, fat is filling as it delays gastric emptying. Gastric emptying refers to the stomach contents being emptied into the small intestines for further digestion and absorption. If you delay gastric emptying, you increase the amount of time you feel full. Simple carbohydrates race through the body and are quickly transformed into sugar and are absorbed. Fat on the other hand takes more time to digest and thus creates a feeling of fullness for a longer duration. This may reduce intake frequency thus promoting weight loss.

Other keto diet health benefits may include improved insulin sensitivity, increased HDL (good cholesterol) levels, reduced acne (secondary to lower insulin levels), and slow tumor growth in specific cancers. This diet is suitable for those looking to lose weight and reduce chronic disease risk.

KETOGENIC DIET FOODS TO INCLUDE/EXCLUDE

The foods included in a keto diet are high in fat and low in carbohydrates. The following list is meant to be comprehensive but may not include all foods that are compatible or incompatible with this diet. Be sure to read the nutrition facts on the back of food items you wish to incorporate before integrating them into your meal plan.

Foods to include:

1. *Meat* – Choose minimally processed organic, grass-fed options. Note: aside from fat, meat is also high in protein, therefore be mindful of intake as too much protein can be converted into glucose in the body ultimately compromising ketosis.
2. *Eggs* – Can be prepared in any way. Prepare in butter to increase fat content.
3. *Fish* – Fatty fish in particular are excellent choices, these include: mackerel, lake trout, sardines, salmon, tuna, and herring (Avoid breading).

4. *Natural fats* – Include plenty of olive oil, coconut oil, butter, and high-fat sauces (be mindful of carbohydrate content).

5. *Non-starchy vegetables* – Low-carb vegetables include: leafy greens, cabbage, zucchini, broccoli, cauliflower, asparagus, and avocado. These foods items pair well with olive oil, or other sources of fat.

6. *High-fat dairy* – Choose high fat cheeses, heavy cream, butter, and high-fat plain yogurt (sweetened yogurts contain too much sugar).

7. *Nuts* – Be mindful of portion sizes of nuts. These are OK to consume on a keto diet, as long as you are mindful of serving size and carb amounts. Pecans, walnuts, and macadamia nuts contain lower amounts of carbohydrates.

8. *Drinks* – Water is preferred. Forgo sugar in coffee, unflavored cream is OK. Unsweetened teas and coconut milk are suitable options.

Foods to avoid:

1. *Sugar* – Sugar can be found in most food items and you must be vigilant when reading food labels. Look at the serving size, carbohydrate, and sugar content of each food item. Foods highest in sugar include: sodas, regular juices, sweet teas, sports drinks, cookies, cakes, condiments, breakfast cereals, pastries, etc.

2. *Starch* – These include but are not limited to: rices, pastas, bagels, breads, French fries, potatoes, chips, oatmeal, beans, lentils, etc.

3. *Beer* – High in carbohydrates which are readily converted into glucose. Avoid.

4. *Fruit* – Contain high amounts of fructose, a natural sugar.

   Tip:

   Avoid foods labeled "Atkins" or foods that are labeled as low-carb alternatives to high-carb foods such as low-carb cookies, cakes, pastries, etc. as most of these food items may contain questionable additives and hidden forms of carbohydrates. It is best to prepare your own food as you will know exactly what it contains in terms of additives, fat, and carbohydrates.

SIMPLIFY KETO WITH INSTANT POT

Preparing meals at home is the best way to ensure you remain in ketosis while optimizing the nutrient profile of your meals. The Instant Pot is a 7-in-1 cooking appliance that can function as a slow cooker, pressure cooker, rice cooker, yogurt maker, steamer, sauté/browning pan, and warming pot. Is the Instant Pot safe? Of course! It has ten proven safety mechanisms to ensure peace of mind versus older, outdated pressure cookers. Why an Instant Pot for my keto diet versus a crock pot? The Instant Pot can reduce cooking time by as much as 70%! This saved time is essential for those with busy lifestyles. Furthermore, pressure cookers are the second most energy efficient cooking appliance after the microwave. The Instant Pot cooks all foods evenly making meats tender and juicy and retains nutrients that would otherwise be lost in water when boiling, steaming, etc. Therefore the inclusion of vegetables in the Instant Pot creates a nutrient packed super meal ready to eat in no time! For those wishing to kick-start their weight loss with delicious, nutritious, easy to prepare keto meals, the Instant Pot is a must have.

DESSERTS

BREAKFAST

COCONUT AND PECAN PORRIDGE

INGREDIENTS

- 1 cup unsweetened dried coconut
- 2 cups unsweetened coconut milk
- 2 2/3 cups water
- 1/4 cup coconut flour
- 1/3 cup ground flaxseed
- 1 tsp vanilla extract
- 1/4 tsp nutmeg
- 1/4 cup chopped pecans or walnuts
- 2 Tbsp maple syrup (*see recipe below)

Nutritional Information

334 Total Calories | 26 g Fat - 234 Calories | 18g Carbs - 72 Calories | 7g Protein - 28 Calories

1. Set Instant Pot to sauté mode and toast coconut until golden in color. Be careful not to burn.

2. Stir in water, coconut milk, coconut flour, and flaxseed.

3. Place lid on pot and set to seal. Cook on high pressure for 3 minutes.

4. Do a quick pressure release and then add vanilla extract and nutmeg. Stir until mixed thoroughly.

5. Portion out porridge into bowls and top with pecans and maple syrup.

KETO MAPLE SYRUP

- 2 ¼ tsp coconut oil
- 1 Tbsp unsalted butter
- ¼ tsp xanthan gum
- ¼ cup powdered erythritol
- ¾ cup water
- ½ tsp vanilla extract
- 2 tsp maple extract

Nutritional Information

99 Total Calories | 11 g Fat - 99 Calories | 0 g Carbs - 0 Calories | 0 g Protein - 0 Calories

---

DIRECTIONS

1. Mix butter, coconut oil, and xanthan gum together in a microwave safe container. Microwave for 40-50 seconds.

2. If the mixture is too thick, add more water.

3. Add vanilla extract and maple extract until desired taste is achieved. Add more water if it needs to be thinned. At this step you can also add more erythritol if you desire a sweeter syrup.

4. Microwave again for 40-60 seconds and then stir. If you prefer hot syrup, then immediately pour on to your meal. If you prefer cool syrup, then let cool and use later.

CINNAMON FRENCH TOAST

INGREDIENTS

- 2 large slices Keto bread
- 1 large egg
- 1 Tbsp coconut cream
- 1/2 tsp cinnamon
- 1/4 tsp Vanilla extract
- 1/4 cup pecans, chopped
- 2 Tbsp butter
- 1 Tbsp sugar-free maple syrup
- 1 tsp stevia brown sugar

Nutritional Information

410 Total Calories | 38 g Fat - 342 Calories | 9 g Carbs - 36 Calories | 8 g Protein - 32 Calories

1. Cut each slice of bread into 4 sticks.

2. Beat together egg, cinnamon, stevia brown sugar, vanilla, and heavy cream.

3. Set Instant Pot to low heat and add butter to pot.

4. Dip sticks into egg mixture and then place in pot.

5. Cook until brown on all sides.

6. Once done, top with butter, cinnamon, chopped pecans, and sugar free syrup.

MINI EGG OMELETS

Prep time: 10 minutes • **Cook time: 20 minutes**

INGREDIENTS

- 4 turkey bacon strips
- 4 large eggs
- 1/2 cup low-sodium cottage cheese
- 1/4 cup heavy cream
- 1-2 cups onions, bell peppers, mushrooms, tomatoes
- 1 ½ cups shredded cheddar cheese
- Siracha or other hot sauce (optional)

Nutritional Information

327 Total Calories | 23 g Fat - 207 Calories | 9 g Carbs - 36 Calories | 21 g Protein - 84 Calories

1. Set Instant Pot to saute mode and book the bacon until crispy. Then, let the pot cool and rinse inside thoroughly.

2. In a blender add eggs, cottage cheese, cheese, heavy cream, and blend until smooth.

3. In a medium bowl, combine bacon, egg mixture, and veggies. Once everything is combined, evenly distribute into mason jars and place lids on top (do not screw on) or you can use foil instead. NOTE: spray jars with cooking spray, unless using silicon molds.

4. Add 1 cup water at bottom of pot. Place steamer basket/trivet in pot and sit jars on top.

5. Place lid on Instant Pot and seal. Set pot to steam for 8 minutes.

6. Allow pressure to naturally release (approx. 10 minutes) and then do a quick release.

7. Remove jars from pot and let cool.

8. Feel free to add Siracha or other hot sauce on top and enjoy!

PEANUT BUTTER AND COCONUT HOT CEREAL

Prep time: 5 minutes • **Cook time: 5 minutes**

INGREDIENTS

- 4 Tbsp coconut, shredded
- 4 tsp almond flour
- 1/2 cup coconut milk
- 1/2 cup water
- 2 Tbsp ground flaxseed
- 2 Tbsp peanut butter
- 1 Tbsp sugar-free maple syrup*

Nutritional Information

332 Total Calories | 28 g Fat - 252 Calories | 13 g Carbs - 52 Calories | 7 g Protein - 28 Calories

1. Turn Instant Pot to saute mode and toast shredded coconut, be careful not to burn.

2. Add almond flour, coconut milk, water, and flaxseed. Stir well.

3. Cover pot with lid, seal vent, and cook on manual high pressure for 2 minutes, then do a quick pressure release.

4. Add sweetener (if desired) and stir until mixed.

5. Portion into bowls and top with peanut butter and sugarfree.

   *NOTE: You can use the maple syrup recipe from the

   coconut and pecan porridge recipe

PEANUT BUTTER PANCAKES

INGREDIENTS

- 2 Tbsp Ghee butter
- 1/4 tsp salt
- 1 tsp baking soda
- 1 Tbsp apple cider vinegar
- 1 tsp vanilla extract
- 1 large egg
- 1 cup almond flour
- 1 cup heavy cream
- 2 Tbsp peanut butter
- 1 Tbsp sugar-free maple syrup

Nutritional Information

376 Total Calories | 36 g Fat - 324 Calories | 8 g Carbs - 32 Calories | 5 g Protein - 20 Calories

DIRECTIONS

1. Beat egg in a bowl, then whisk in salt and baking soda.

2. Add apple cider vinegar, stir until combined.

3. Add vanilla extract and cream, mix.

4. Add almond flour, whisk until smooth.

5. Set Instant Pot to manual low pressure and melt butter in bottom of pot.

6. Drop in some of pancake batter (may be best to use ladle) and cook for

2 minutes each side, until slightly brown

7. Once done, place on plate and spread butter, peanut butter, and sugar-free syrup

   on top

   NOTE: You can also top with heavy whipped cream and berries

SPINACH AND BACON CHEESY EGG MUFFIN

Prep time: 5 minutes • **Cook time: 10 minutes**

INGREDIENTS

- 4 large eggs
- 2 Tbsp unsweetened coconut milk
- 1/8 tsp black pepper
- 1 Tbsp chopped bacon, pre-cooked
- 1 Tbsp shredded cheddar cheese
- 1 Tbsp spinach, finely chopped
- 1 tsp chopped scallions
- 1/2 avocado, sliced
- Lemon juice (to taste)

Nutritional Information

246 Total Calories | 18 g Fat - 162 Calories | 5 g Carbs - 20 Calories |16 g Protein - 64 Calories

1. In a small bowl, whisk together eggs and milk.

2. Pour mixture evenly into silicone cupcake molds (only fill 1/2 of the way full).

3. Top with bacon, spinach, scallions, and cheese.

4. Pour 1 cup water into Instant Pot, insert trivet, place molds onto trivet and cover pot with lid. Seal vent.

5. Set Instant Pot to manual high pressure, cook for 5 minutes.

6. Once done, do a quick release and remove eggs from mold.

7. Top eggs with additional cheese and then pair with sliced avocado that is seasoned with lemon juice and black pepper.

BACON AND EGG BREAKFAST BAKE

Prep time: 10 minutes • **Cook time: 20 minutes**

INGREDIENTS

- 6 large eggs
- 6 slices bacon
- 1/4 cup unsweetened coconut milk
- 1/2 cup shredded cheddar cheese
- 1/2 tsp pepper
- 1/4 cup onion, chopped
- 1/4 cup mushrooms
- 1 tsp Siracha

Nutritional Information

293 Total Calories | 21 g Fat - 189 Calories | 4 g Carbs - 16 Calories | 22 g Protein - 88 Calories

DIRECTIONS

1. Set Instant Pot to saute mode
2. Dice bacon and place into pot, cook until crispy
3. Add chopped vegetables and saute for approx. 2-3 mins (can add additional if you prefer).
4. In a medium bowl, whisk together eggs, pepper, cheese, and milk
5. Add bacon and veggies into egg mixture and stir to combine
6. Grease a Pyrex dish that fits into Instant Pot
7. Pour mixture into Pyrex dish
8. Pour 1-2 cups water into Instant Pot, insert steamer basket/trivet in pot, and place dish on trivet
9. Cover pot with lid and cook on manual high pressure for 20 minutes, then do a quick release
10. Serve topped with Siracha and more cheese

BLUEBERRY AND LEMON BREAKFAST MUFFIN

Prep time: 15 minutes • **Cook time: 40 minutes**

INGREDIENTS

- 1/2 cup almond flour
- 1/4 tsp salt
- 1/2 tsp baking soda
- 1/4 cup unsalted butter
- 1/2 cup Monk fruit Stevia blend
- 1/2 tsp vanilla extract
- 4 large eggs
- 1/4 cup blueberries
- 1 Tbsp fresh squeezed lemon juice

Nutritional Information

234 Total Calories | 18 g Fat - 162 Calories | 11 g Carbs - 44 Calories | 7 g Protein - 28 Calories

---

DIRECTIONS

1. Grease cake pan that fits into Instant Pot

2. Mix together almond flour, salt, and baking soda. Set aside half for later (you will use it with the blueberries).

3. In a separate bowl beat together lemon juice, sweetener, and butter.

4. Add vanilla and egg to butter mixture and combine.

5. Gradually add flour mixture to the butter mixture and stir until thoroughly combined.

6. Carefully toss blueberries in the flour mixture that was set aside from step 2. Fold into flour mixture from step 5

7. Add 2/3 cup water to Instant Pot. Pour batter into greased pan

8. Place trivet into Instant Pot and place pan on top. Cover and cook on manual high pressure for 30 minutes

9. Once done, do quick release. Serve and enjoy

SIDES, APPETIZERS, AND SNACKS

SIMPLE YOGURT

Prep time: 5 minutes • **Cook time: 15 hours**

INGREDIENTS

- 3 14oz cans coconut cream
- 1 envelope yogurt starter

Topping options:
- cinnamon
- peanut butter
- berries
- vanilla extract
- Chopped nuts

Nutritional Information

329 Total Calories | 33 g Fat - 297 Calories | 5 g Carbs - 20 Calories | 3 g Protein - 12 Calories

1. Set Instant Pot to "yogurt" mode and adjust until it displays boil.

2. Pour cream into pot and cover with lid.

3. Allow pot to heat up. Once pot beeps (meaning boil temp reached), pour in yogurt starter and whisk

4. Replace lid and set to "yogurt" mode again and adjust time to 15 hours

5. Once done, divide yogurt into jars and place in refrigerator. Let chill for 12-24 hrs.

6. When ready to eat, top with peanut butter, cinnamon, berries, or vanilla.

CAULIFLOWER MASH

Prep time: 5 minutes • **Cook time: 15 hours**

INGREDIENTS

- 1 large cauliflower head
  (core and cut into large chunks)
- 1 cup chicken or vegetable broth
- 2 Tbsp butter
- ½ tsp ground black pepper and salt (to taste)
- ¾ - 1 cup grated parmesan cheese

DIRECTIONS

1. Place steamer basket/trivet in pot and add cauliflower and broth.

2. Cover with lid and set valve to sealing.

3. Cook for 3-5 minutes on high.

4. Once done, quick release the pressure.

5. Place cauliflower in food processor and add butter, salt, pepper, and cheese. Blend until smooth. NOTE: if you do not have a food processor, then remove trivet and cauliflower in order to drain the liquid from Instant Pot. Add the cauliflower back to pot with butter, salt, pepper, and cheese. Use an immersion blender to puree until smooth.

6. Best if served immediately.

SIMPLE CAULIFLOWER RICE

Prep time: 5-10 minutes • **Cook time: 20 minutes**

INGREDIENTS

- 1 cup water
- 1 large head of cauliflower, washed, cored, cut into large chunks (make sure to trim leaves)
- 2 Tbsp extra virgin olive oil or butter
- ¼ tsp salt (may need more per personal preference)

Nutritional Information

123 Total Calories | 7 g Fat - 63 Calories | 11 g Carbs - 44 Calories | 4 g Protein - 16 Calories

DIRECTIONS

1. Pour water into Instant Pot.

2. Place steamer basket into pot and put cauliflower chunks in basket.

3. Cover with lid and set vent to seal.

4. Set pot to manual pressure for 1 minute (please note it will take approximately 10 minutes for the pot to get to pressure, so be patient).

5. Once done cooking, do a quick pressure release and remove cauliflower from pot.

6. Press cancel on pot, pour out the water, and then reset pot to sauté mode.

7. Once pot is hot, add oil (or butter) to pot and allow it to heat up. Then add cauliflower.

8. As cauliflower is sautéing, use a fork or potato masher to break up the cauliflower to desired consistency.

9. Add salt and other seasonings of your choice.

10. Eat it as is or serve with any of the other great recipes provided!

SPICED UP RED CABBAGE

Prep time: 5 minutes • **Cook time: 10 minutes**

INGREDIENTS

- 3 Tbsp butter (avocado oil or coconut oil can also be used)
- 3 cloves garlic, minced
- 2 tsp ground allspice (or ground nutmeg)
- 8 cups shredded red cabbage
- 1 tsp salt
- 1/2 tsp pepper
- 1/3 cup water

Nutritional Information

78 Total Calories | 6 g Fat - 54 Calories | 5 g Carbs - 20 Calories | 1 g Protein - 4 Calories

1. Set Instant Pot to sauté mode and add butter (or oil). Once pot is hot, add garlic and allspice, mix thoroughly.

2. Add remaining ingredients and place lid on pot. Set vent to seal.

3. Set pot on manual and cook for 5 minutes, then do a quick release.

4. Mix one last time before serving, enjoy!

STUFFED CABBAGE ROLLS

Prep time: 10 minutes • **Cook time: 20 minutes**

INGREDIENTS

- 1 large cabbage head
- 2 Tbsp butter
- 1 cup yellow onion, chopped
- 3 cloves garlic, minced
- 1/2 tsp black pepper
- 1 lb ground turkey
- 1 can diced tomatoes, drained
- 32 oz tomato soup

Nutritional Information

393 Total Calories | 13 g Fat - 153 Calories | 24 g Carbs - 120 Calories | 23 g Protein - 112 Calories

1. Core the cabbage and remove outer leaves.

2. Pour one cup of water in the Instant Pot and place trivet in pot. Place head of cabbage on trivet.

3. Set pot to manual high pressure and cook for 10 minutes and then do a quick release.

4. Remove cabbage and let cool completely.

5. Turn Instant Pot to sauté mode and add butter. Once butter is heated, add garlic onions, ground turkey, salt, and pepper and sauté until meat browns.

6. Once browned, add diced tomatoes and mix thoroughly.

7. To make the rolls, remove whole cabbage leaves and lay flat on counter and place 2 Tbsp of meat mixture in the center of leaf, until entire mixture is used.

8. Roll up the cabbage and tuck in sides (like a burrito).

9. Pour 16 ounces of tomato soup and 1 cup of water into pot. Add cabbage rolls (it is ok to layer them). Then add the rest of the soup and top with the diced tomatoes.

10. Cover with lid and seal vent.

11. Set pot to manual high pressure for 10 minutes, then do a quick pressure release.

12. Serve on top of cauliflower mash with butter and enjoy!

SWEET AND SPICY CHICKEN WINGS

INGREDIENTS

- 1 lb chicken wings
- 2 Tbsp avocado oil
- 1/2 tsp salt
- 1/4 cup sugar-free honey
- 2 tsp Siracha
- 1/4 cup water

Optional:
1/2 tsp garlic powder (can add
with the salt, or can use garlic salt)

Nutritional Information

353 Total Calories | 25 g Fat - 225 Calories | 11 g Carbs - 44 Calories | 21 g Protein - 84 Calories

DIRECTIONS

1. Pat chicken wings dry and lightly sprinkle with salt.

2. Whisk together Siracha and honey and use half of mixture to cover chicken (can brush liquid onto chicken).

3. Turn Instant Pot to sauté mode and add avocado oil. Once pot is hot, add chicken wings and brown each side for approx. 2 minutes. Be careful as these will burn quickly.

4. Once chicken is done browning, add water and place lid on pot. Set vent to seal and turn pot to manual high pressure for 5 minutes.

5. Do a quick release and carefully remove lid.

6. Remove wings and place onto plate or serving platter. Pour remaining Siracha and honey mixture over wings.

MUSHROOM RISOTTO

INGREDIENTS

- 1 large head cauliflower, washed cored, and grated
- 2 Tbsp coconut oil
- 1 medium yellow onion, diced
- 1 lb shitake mushrooms, sliced
- 4 cloves garlic, minced
- 2-3 Tbsp coconut aminos
- 1 cup coconut milk
- 1 cup low-sodium chicken broth
- 1/4 cup nutritional yeast
- 1/2 tsp pink salt
- 1-2 Tbsp xanthun gum
- 1/2 tsp black pepper

Nutritional Information

274 Total Calories | 18 g Fat - 162 Calories | 15 g Carbs - 60 Calories | 13 g Protein - 52 Calories

DIRECTIONS

1. Grate cauliflower with food processor (with grater attachment) or use cheese grater.

2. Set Instant Pot to saute mode and add coconut oil

3. Once oil is hot, add mushrooms, onions, and garlic, stirring occasionally. Saute until mushrooms are tender (approx. 5-7 minutes)

4. Add coconut aminos and continue to saute until onions and mushrooms are brown (approx. 5 minutes)

5. Turn pot off and add coconut milk, broth, cauliflower rice, salt, and nutritional yeast. Stir until combined

6. Cover pot with lid, seal vent, and set to manual pressure for 2 minutes

7. Do a quick pressure release and gradually add xanthun gum to thicken

8. Add salt and pepper to taste, serve, and enjoy!

LEMON AND PARMESAN ZOODLES

Prep time: 10 minutes • **Cook time: 5 minutes**

INGREDIENTS

- 2 Tbsp extra virgin olive oil
- 2-3 cloves of garlic, minced
- Zest of ½ lemon
- 1/2 tsp salt
- 2 large zucchinis, spiralized
- Juice of 1/3 lemon
- 1/4 cup grated Parmesan cheese
- Pepper to taste
- 13 oz canned and drained artichokes (optional)

Nutritional Information

171 Total Calories | 11 g Fat - 99 Calories | 12 g Carbs - 48 Calories | 6 g Protein - 24 Calories

DIRECTIONS

1. Set Instant Pot to sauté mode. Once hot, add olive oil, salt, lemon zest, and garlic. Stir occasionally and cook for approx. 1-2 minutes.

2. Add spiralized zucchini and lemon juice, stirring continuously to coat the noodles with the olive oil that is already in pot.

3. If you choose to add artichokes, then this would be the step to do so.

4. Once zoodles and artichokes are warmed through, add Parmesan cheese and pepper. Mix again to combine.

5. Add additional salt and pepper to taste, along with a Tbsp of butter or diced avocado.

SAUCY TURKEY MEATBALLS

Prep time: 10 minutes • **Cook time: 20 minutes**

INGREDIENTS

- 1-1 ½ lb ground turkey
- ½ cup almond flour
- 1 large egg, room temperature 1/4 tsp salt
- 2 garlic cloves, minced
- 6 Tbsp butter (will be divided in recipe)
- 6 Tbsp Frank's Red Hot sauce
  (or preferred hot sauce)

Nutritional Information

299 Total Calories | 23 g Fat - 207 Calories | 1 g Carbs - 4 Calories | 22 g Protein - 88 Calories

DIRECTIONS

1. Add turkey, almond flour, egg, salt, and garlic to a large bowl. Combine all these ingredients with your hands (do not overwork the meat).

2. Grease your hands with oil and roll meat mixture into individual balls (approx. 1-2 inches wide).

3. Turn Instant Pot to sauté mode and add 2 Tbsp butter.

4. Add a few meatballs until the bottom is covered and cook until all sides are brown. *NOTE: you will need to do this in several batches as you will do one layer at a time to ensure even browning of meatballs (approx. 2 minutes a side).

5. As your meatballs are in the pot, add your choice of hot sauce and 4 Tbsp of butter in a microwave safe container and microwave until butter is melted. Stir occasionally.

6. Once all of your meatballs are browned, add them all back into pot and pour your hot sauce mixture over them. Cover with lid and seal vent.

7. Set pot to manual high pressure for 10 minutes. Once done cooking, naturally release pressure for 5 minutes and then quick release the remaining pressure.

8. Serve as is or pair with cheesy cauliflower mash!

DECONSTRUCTED DEVILED EGGS

INGREDIENTS

- 10 large eggs
- 5 strips bacon, raw
- 2 Tbsp mayonnaise (see next page for recipe)
- 1/4 tsp smoked paprika
- 1 stalk green onion

Nutritional Information

182 Total Calories | 14 g Fat - 126 Calories | 1 g Carbs - 4 Calories | 13 g Protein - 52 Calories

DIRECTIONS

1. This recipe requires a cake pan that will fit into Instant Pot while sitting on steaming basket/trivet (6-7" pan).

2. Liberally grease the entire inside of cake pan.

3. Crack open eggs in the cake pan – do not whisk or stir eggs. Try not to break the yolks (it is ok if some accidentally break)

4. Pour a cup of cold water into the bottom of the Instant Pot, place the steam rack in pot, and set the cake pan on top of it.

5. Place lid on Instant Pot and set steam vent to seal. Cook on high pressure for 6 minutes.

6. Naturally release pressure for 10 minutes.

7. Remove cake pan from pot and blot off any moisture from the top of the eggs.

8. Remove egg loaf from pan (easiest way is to turn pan over on cutting board to release the egg loaf). Roughly chop eggs and scoop into a mixing bowl.

9. Clean the inner bowl of pot and then place it back inside the base of the Instant Pot. Set to sauté on medium heat. Chop up the slices of bacon, then add it to the pot and cook until crispy.

10. Add the bacon and the rendered fat to mixing bowl containing the chopped eggs.

11. Add mayonnaise, smoked paprika, and any additional salt, pepper, or mus-tard if you desire. Toss to combine.

12. Garnish with chopped green onion, serve, and enjoy!

MAYONNAISE FOR DECONSTRUCTED DEVILED EGGS

INGREDIENTS

- 1 large egg (room temp)
- 2 large egg yolks (room temp)
- ¼ tsp salt
- ¼ tsp pepper
- 1-2 tsp Dijon mustard
- ¾ cup extra virgin olive oil
- ½ cup coconut oil

Nutritional Information

193 Total Calories | 21 g Fat - 189 Calories | 0 g Carbs - 0 Calories | 1 g Protein - 4 Calories

DIRECTIONS

1. Add all ingredients to bowl and use immersion blender to mix thoroughly.

2. Once blended, add to recipe as instructed.

   RECIPE NOTE: Feel free to add more mustard, salt and pepper per your preference, just make sure to add gradually.

   **Consuming raw or undercooked meats, poultry, seafood, shellfish, or eggs may increase your risk of food borne illness.

BUTTERY MASHED CAULIFLOWER

INGREDIENTS

- 1 large head of cauliflower
- 1 cup water
- 1/4 cup half and half
- 1-2 Tbsp unsalted butter
- Salt & pepper to taste

Nutritional Information

140 total calories | 8 g fat - 72 calories | 12 g carbs - 48 calories | 5 g Protein - 20 calories

DIRECTIONS

1. Wash, core, and roughly chop cauliflower into large chunks.

2. Pour water into Instant Pot and insert steaming rack and basket. Place cauliflower chunks on rack.

3. Place lid and set vent to seal. Set on manual high pressure for 3-5 minutes.

4. After timer complete, allow pressure to release naturally.

5. Remove and drain cauliflower.

6. Add cauliflower and remaining ingredients into food processor while cauliflower is still warm and blend to desired consistency. Add more salt and pepper to taste (if desired).

7. Serve and enjoy!

SOUP, STEW, AND CHILI

CREAMY JALAPEÑO CHICKEN SOUP

INGREDIENTS

- 1 lb chicken (boneless, skinless)
- 3 Tbsp Ghee butter
- 1/2 onion, chopped
- 2 jalapeños, diced and seeded
- 1/2 lb bacon
- 3 cups low-sodium chicken broth
- 1/2 cup heavy whipping cream
- 1/4 tsp paprika
- 1 tsp cumin
- 1/2 tsp black pepper
- 1 1/2 cup shredded cheddar cheese
- 1/2 tsp xanthun gum

Nutritional Information

471 Total Calories | 35 g Fat - 315 Calories | 4 g Carbs - 16 Calories | 35 g Protein - 140 Calories

DIRECTIONS

1. Set Instant Pot to saute mode,. Cook bacon until crispy.

2. Remove bacon from pot and rinse thoroughly.

3. Turn pot back to saute mode and add butter. Once hot, add onions, jalapeños, paprika, cumin, and black pepper.

4. Once onions are tender, add broth, chicken (cubed), and cream cheese.

5. Set pot to manual high pressure and cook for 15 minutes.

6. Once done, do a natural pressure release for 5 minutes and then do a quick release.

7. Shred chicken and then turn pot back to saute mode.

8. Add cheese, heavy whipping cream, and cooked bacon. Stir until cheese melts and then add xanthun gum.

9. Once cheese is melted, turn pot to warm and simmer until liquid thickens

10. Serve and top with additional bacon, cheese, green onions.

SPICY BUFFALO CHICKEN SOUP

Prep time: 5-10 minutes • **Cook time: 15 minutes**

INGREDIENTS

- 2 lbs boneless skinless chicken breast
- 3 cups low-sodium chicken broth
- 1/2 celery, diced
- 1/4 cup yellow onion, diced
- 2 cloves garlic, minced
- 2 Tbsp butter
- 1/3 cup Frank's Red Hot sauce
- 2 cups shredded cheddar cheese
- 1 cup heavy cream

Nutritional Information

339 Total Calories | 23 g Fat - 207 Calories | 4 g Carbs - 16 Calories | 29 g Protein - 116 Calories

DIRECTIONS

1. Set Instant Pot to saute mode and add butter.

2. Once pot is hot, add celery, garlic, and onion.

3. Saute for approx. 2 minutes (until onions are soft).

4. Add chicken and broth to pot.

5. Cover pot with lid and seal vent.

6. Set pot to manual high pressure and cook for 10 minutes. Do a quick release.

7. Once done cooking, shred chicken and set pot to "keep warm".

8. Add cream cheese and heavy cream and stir until melted.

9. Serve and top with cheddar cheese.

TACO SOUP

INGREDIENTS

- 2 lbs ground beef
- 3 cloves garlic, minced
- 1 Tbsp onion powder
- 1 Tbsp chili powder
- 2 tsp cumin
- 1 can diced tomatoes with green chiles
- 32 oz beef broth or bone broth
- 8 oz cream cheese
- 1/2 cup heavy cream
- Diced jalapeños
- Shredded cheddar cheese Sour cream

Nutritional Information

436 Total Calories | 32 g Fat - 288 Calories | 7 g Carbs - 28 Calories | 30 g Protein - 120 Calories

1. Set Instant Pot to sauté mode. Once pot is hot, add ground beef and cook until slightly browned.

2. Once meat is browned, add onion powder, chili powder, garlic, cumin, broth, and the tomatoes.

3. Stir mixture together and place lid on pot. Set vent to seal and place pot to the soup setting.

4. Cook for 7 minutes and then let pressure naturally release for 10 minutes and then quick release remaining pressure.

5. Turn pot to the keep warm setting and add cream cheese and heavy cream, mix until cream cheese is melted.

6. Portion out into serving bowls and top with cheese, jalapeños, and sour cream. NOTE: can also use bacon as a topper (cook as you normally do and crumble on top).

CHEESEBURGER SOUP

Prep time: 15 minutes • **Cook time: 15 minutes**

INGREDIENTS

- 6 oz bacon
- 1 ½ lb ground turkey
- 1 Tbsp olive oil
- 1 large onion, chopped
- 2 large carrots, diced
- 2 stalks celery, diced
- 4 cups cauliflower, chopped
- 4 cups bone broth
- 4 oz cream cheese
- 1 ½ cup shredded sharp cheddar cheese

Nutritional Information

408 total calories | 28 g fat - 252 calories | 7 g carbs - 28 calories | 32 g Protein - 128 calories

DIRECTIONS

1. Set Instant Pot to sauté and brown sausage. Once browned, remove from pot.

2. Place ground turkey in pot and brown until cooked through, remove.

3. Add olive oil, carrots, celery, onion, and cauliflower to pot and sauté to soften.

4. Pour in bone broth and place lid on pot and seal.

5. Set to manual for 7 minutes, and then do a quick release.

6. Keep vegetables and broth in pot and puree with an immersion blender.

7. Add cheese and blend again to mix.

8. Stir in the bacon and ground turkey, let sit for a few minutes.

9. Once warmed through, serve in bowl and top with additional cheese.

CHICKEN CHILI

Prep time: 5 minutes • **Cook time: 20 minutes**

INGREDIENTS

- 3-4 frozen boneless, skinless chicken breast
- 1/2 large onion, chopped
- 1 cup water or low-sodium broth
- 2 15 oz cans diced tomatoes (do not drain)
- 1 6 oz can tomato paste
- 1 4 oz can green chiles (do not drain)
- 1/2 cup chili powder
- 1 tsp garlic powder
- 2 Tbsp cumin
- 1 Tbsp dried oregano
- 2 tsp salt
- 2 tsp ground black pepper

Toppings:
Avocado
Sour cream
Shredded cheddar cheese

Nutritional Information

364 total calories | 12 g fat - 108 calories | 27 g carbs - 108 calories | 37 g Protein - 148 calories

DIRECTIONS

1. Place chopped onions in the bottom of the Instant Pot.

2. Lay chicken breast on top of onions.

3. Add ingredients from the water to the pepper.

4. Place lid on pot and select soup (or stew) and cook for 8-10 minutes. Once done, let pressure naturally release for approx. 10 minutes.

5. If internal temperature of chicken is at least 165 degrees F, then remove chicken to shred and then add back to Instant Pot. Mix shredded chicken and other ingredients in pot until combined evenly.

6. Portion out into serving bowls and top with diced avocado, sour cream, and shredded cheddar cheese.

MEALS
AND
ENTREES

ASIAN CHICKEN

Prep time: 10 minutes • **Cook time: 20 minutes**

INGREDIENTS

- 2 cups water
- 2 lbs boneless, skinless chicken
- thighs (cut into large chunks)
- 2 Tbsp coconut aminos
- 1 Tbsp sesame oil
- 1 Tbsp ginger, minced
- 1 Tbsp garlic, minced
- 4 tsp Swerve or similar sweetener
- 1 Tbsp rice vinegar
- 1/4 cup Julienned carrots
- 1/4 cup Julienned red bell peppers
- 1/4 cup chopped red onions
- 1/3 cup peanuts, crushed

Nutritional Information

268 Total Calories | 12 g Fat - 108 Calories | 8 g Carbs - 32 Calories | 32 g Protein - 128 Calories

DIRECTIONS

1. Combine all ingredients into a Pyrex dish (or any other dish that is approved for Instant Pot) and cover with lid.

2. Pour water into Instant Pot and place trivet/steamer basket into pot.

3. Place heat safe dish with ingredients onto steamer basket.

4. Set Instant Pot to manual high pressure for 10 minutes and then do a natural release of the pressure for 10 minutes. After 10 mins, do a quick release for the rest.

5. Shred chicken (can either do so while inside of pot or remove and shred on plate).

6. Serve over cauliflower rice and top with a tablespoon of butter.

   *NOTE: if you want your vegetables and peanuts to remain crunchy, then add them to the dish after the remaining ingredients have finished cooking. You can also top with a fried egg.

AVOCADO AND STEAK FAJITA BOWL

INGREDIENTS

- 2 lbs fajita steak strips, cubed
- 1 Tbsp water
- 2-3 cloves garlic, minced
- 1 Tbsp extra virgin olive oil
- 2 tsp lime juice (can use fresh squeezed or bottled)
- 2 bell peppers, sliced or diced
- 1/2 tsp chili powder
- 1/2 tsp salt
- 1/2 tsp black pepper
- 1 tsp tabasco (or other chipotle sauce)
- 3 ripe avocados, diced

Nutritional Information

351 Total Calories | 19 g Fat - 171 Calories | 12 g Carbs - 48 Calories | 33 g Protein - 132 Calories

DIRECTIONS

1. Set Instant Pot to sauté mode and add olive oil, let heat up.

2. Add garlic and cook until slightly brown, but be careful not to burn.

3. Once garlic is browned, add all ingredients except the avocado. Stir to combine ingredients evenly.

4. Cover with lid and set vent to seal. Set Instant Pot to manual high pressure for 10 minutes.

5. Once done cooking, do a quick release and remove lid (carefully).

6. If you want the dish to have more liquid, then you can serve on diced avocado at this point. If you want less liquid, then go to step #7.

7. Turn your Instant Pot back to sauté mode and sauté until the liquid is reduced to half or slightly less, stirring occasionally so mixture does not burn.

8. Once liquid reduced, portion avocado into bowls and serve steak mixture on top.

9. You can also add other toppings, such as: shredded cheddar cheese, sour cream, diced tomatoes, and cilantro.

BALSAMIC ROAST BEEF

INGREDIENTS

- 3 pounds chuck roast
- 1 Tbsp avocado oil (or olive oil)
- 1 Tbsp coconut aminos
- 3 cloves garlic, crushed
- 1 cup beef broth
- 1 tsp salt
- 1/2 tsp black ground pepper
- 2 Tbsp butter
- 1/2 tsp thyme
- 1/4 cup balsamic vinegar
- 1/2 tsp rosemary
- 1/4 cup scallions

Nutritional Information

264 Total Calories | 12 g Fat - 108 Calories | 7 g Carbs - 28 Calories | 32g Protein - 128 Calories

DIRECTIONS

1. Mix together balsamic vinegar, salt, pepper, thyme, garlic, and rosemary. Rub on all sides of roast.

2. Turn Instant Pot to sauté mode on high. One it says "hot", place oil and roast into pot. Sear on all sides (takes about 3-5 minutes per side).

3. Once roast is done browning, remove from pot and deglaze with the butter, broth, and balsamic vinegar. Mix the liquid and browned bits together.

4. Add the roast and coconut aminos to the liquid in the pot. Secure lid and cook on high for 40-45 minutes.

5. Once done cooking, do a quick or natural release and remove the roast to let sit (approx. 5 minutes).

6. While roast is resting, make a glaze by turning the pot to sauté mode and reduce the remaining liquid by two thirds. This will take about 10 minutes.

7. Serve roast with scallions and glaze on top and enjoy!

BEEF STROGANOFF

Prep time: 7-10 minutes • **Cook time: 30 minutes**

INGREDIENTS

- 2 Tbsp coconut oil
- 1/2 cup yellow onion, diced
- 1 Tbsp garlic, minced
- 1 lb beef stew meat
- 1 1/2 cup mushrooms, chopped
- 1 Tsp coconut aminos
- 1 tsp salt
- 1 tsp black pepper
- 3/4 cup water
- 1/3 cup sour cream
- 1/4 tsp xanthun gum

Nutritional Information

276 Total Calories | 16 g Fat - 144 Calories | 6 g Carbs - 24 Calories | 27 g Protein - 108 Calories

DIRECTIONS

1. Set Instant Pot to saute on high and add oil. Once hot, add onions and garlic and saute until onions are transluscent.

2. After sauteing the onions and garlic for a few minutes, add meat, mushrooms, coconut aminos, salt, pepper, and water.

3. Cover pot with lid, set vent to seal, and turn to manual high pressure and cook for 20 minutes.

4. Once done, let pressure naturally release for 10 minutes and then do a quick release.

5. Turn pot back to saute mode and add sour cream and xanthun gum, stir until liquid thickens.

6. Serve over cauliflower mash or cauliflower rice.

   NOTE: Can also add bacon to recipe. Just omit the oil and cook the bacon first. Once done cooking, remove bacon from pot (leaving grease) and then begin with step #1

CAULIFLOWER AND CHICKEN CASSEROLE

Prep time: 10 minutes • **Cook time: 25 minutes**

INGREDIENTS

- 2 stalks celery, chopped
- 1/2 large yellow onion, diced
- 2 cloves garlic, minced
- 1 head cauliflower, washed, cored, chopped
- 3 Tbsp Ghee butter
- 1 lb breakfast sausage
- 8 oz package cream cheese
- 1 lb cooked chicken, shredded
- 1 cup shredded cheddar cheese
- 1 cup shredded Colby Jack cheese
- 1/2 tsp pepper
- 1/2 tsp paprika
- 1 cup water

Nutritional Information

380 Total Calories | 28 g Fat - 252 Calories | 8 g Carbs - 32 Calories | 24 g Protein - 96 Calories

DIRECTIONS

1. Set Instant Pot to sauté mode.

2. Add butter to pot and let it melt.

3. Sauté celery, onion, and garlic for approx. 3-5 minutes.

4. Add sausage and allow to brown, crumbling it up with the veggies.

5. Add cream cheese and shredded chicken in with your vegetable mixture, and combine together.

6. Put the cauliflower, shredded cheeses, salt, pepper, and paprika on top of the mixture in the Instant Pot.

7. Add 1 cup of water.

8. Put the lid on your Instant Pot and seal vent.

9. Turn Instant Pot to manual high pressure for 8 minutes; allow a natural pressure release for 10 minutes and then do a quick release for remaining pressure.

10. When it's done, stir the casserole together. If there is extra water, turn the sauté function back on and let it cook down just a little bit.

11. Serve and top it off with chopped basil or parsley if desired.

CHIPOTLE BEEF ROAST

Prep time: 10 minutes • **Cook time: 1 hour 30 minutes**

INGREDIENTS

- 1 1/2 lb chuck roast
- 2 Tbsp extra virgin olive oil
- 1 Tbsp cumin
- 1 Tbsp oregano
- 1 tsp onion powder
- 1 tsp chili powder
- 2 tsp garlic, minced
- 1 medium yellow onion, sliced
- 1/2 cup bone broth
- 7 oz can of chipotle peppers
- 14 oz can diced tomatoes
- 2 cups bell peppers, sliced
- 1 jalapeño, diced
- 1 avocado, diced
- 1/4 cup sour cream

Nutritional Information

435 Total Calories | 31 g Fat - 279 Calories | 15 g Carbs - 60 Calories | 24 g Protein - 96 Calories

DIRECTIONS

1. Set Instant Pot to saute mode and add oil.

2. While oil is heating, mix all the spices together, rub on roast.

3. Add meat to pot and brown (approx. 3 minutes per side).

4. Remove meat from pot, add more oil (if needed) and saute onions and garlic. (approx. 2 minutes)

5. Add broth, chipotle peppers, tomatoes, bell peppers, and jalapeño.

6. Stir everything together and then place roast on top.

7. Cover pot with lid, seal vent, and turn pot to manual high pressure.

8. Cook for 45 minutes, then do a quick pressure release.

9. Serve on top of cauliflower rice with avocado and sour cream.

CREAMY RANCH CHICKEN

INGREDIENTS

- 1/2 pound raw bacon, diced
- 2 pounds boneless, skinless chicken breasts
- 10-12 oz of cream cheese
- 4 Tbsp (2 1 oz packets) of dry Ranch seasoning mix
- 1 cup shredded cheddar cheese
- 1 cup water or bone broth
- 1 cup mayonnaise

Optional:
1/4 cup sliced jalapeños
1/4 cup chopped scallions

Nutritional Information

554 Total Calories | 46 g Fat - 414 Calories | 4 g Carbs - 16 Calories | 31 g Protein - 124 Calories

DIRECTIONS

1. Start by setting your Instant Pot to sauté mode on high. Once it says "hot", add bacon and cook until done. Once bacon is finished cooking, turn off instant pot and set the cooked bacon aside for later.

2. Pour liquid into pot and add chicken, cream cheese, and seasoning.

3. Set Instant Pot to poultry mode on high. Cook for 12 minutes.

4. After the time is up, do a natural pressure release for 5 minutes and then a quick release.

5. Remove chicken and shred (leave the remaining ingredients in pot). Once chicken is shredded, place back into Instant Pot and add shredded cheddar cheese, mayonnaise, and bacon.

6. Mix until combined.

7. Place lid back on pot (do not turn on) and let all ingredients sit for approximately 5 minutes. This allows the sauce to thicken.

8. Serve in a bowl and top with sliced jalapeños and scallions.

CREAMY SHRIMP SCAMPI

INGREDIENTS

- 2 Tbsp butter
- 1 lb shrimp, frozen that has been deveined and peeled, leave tail on
- 4 cloves minced garlic
- 1/2 lemon
- ¼- ½ tsp red pepper flakes
- 1/2 tsp paprika
- 1 cup chicken broth
- 1/2 cup half and half
- 1/2 cup parmesan cheese
- Pepper to taste
- Dried parsley to taste

Nutritional Information

320 Total Calories | 20 g Fat - 180 Calories | 5 g Carbs - 20 Calories | 30 g Protein - 120 Calories

DIRECTIONS

1. Turn Instant Pot to sauté mode. Add butter once pot is hot and let melt.

2. Add red pepper and garlic and cook until garlic is browned (1-2 minutes, it only needs to be slightly browned).

3. Add the shrimp, paprika, and pepper (can add more seasonings after cooking if desired).

4. Pour in broth and cover with lid. Place vent to seal.

5. Cook on manual high pressure for 3 minutes and do a quick release.

6. Change to sauté mode and add in cheese and half and half. Stir until cheese is melted and sauce begins to bubble.

7. Add lemon and dried parsley and stir until combined.

8. Serve and enjoy!

CREAMY SUN-DRIED TOMATO AND SPINACH CHICKEN

Prep time: 10 minutes • Cook time: 15 minutes

INGREDIENTS

- 1 lb boneless, skinless chicken breasts (*see seasoning ingredients below)
- 1-2 Tbsp extra virgin olive oil
- 1 cup fresh spinach, chopped
- 1/2 cup heavy whipping cream
- 1/3 cup grated parmesan cheese
- 1/2 cup water or low-sodium chicken broth
- 1/4 cup sun-dried tomatoes, chopped
- 2 Tbsp cream cheese

*Chicken seasoning ingredients:
- 5 cloves minced garlic
- 1 tsp dried basil
- 1 tsp dried oregano
- 1 tsp red pepper flakes
- 1/2 tsp salt
- 1/4 tsp ground black pepper

Nutritional Information

340 total calories | 24 g fat - 216 calories | 5 g carbs - 20 calories | 26 g Protein - 104 calories

DIRECTIONS

1. In a small bowl, combine chicken seasoning ingredients thoroughly.

2. Make the chicken breasts thinner by slicing them in half (horizontally). Lightly pat each side with paper towel, then add seasoning mixture onto each side of chicken breasts.

3. Set Instant Pot to sauté mode on medium heat. Once pot is hot, add olive oil and then careful place chicken into pot (need to place them in a single layer, so may need to do this step twice).

4. Goal is to sauté chicken until golden brown on each side, this will take approx. 2-3 minutes per side. Turn sauté mode off.

5. Keeping chicken in the pot, add water or chicken broth. May need to add more liquid if bottom of pot is not fully covered.

6. Place lid on pot and set vent to seal. Cook on manual high pressure for 5 minutes and then do a quick release.

7. Remove chicken and place on plate. Then cut into strips, and discard half of the remaining liquid left from the pot.

8. Turn pot back onto sauté mode on medium heat and add cream cheese and heavy cream.

9. Let sauce simmer until cream cheese is melted, stirring occasionally.

10. Add spinach, sun-dried tomatoes, and parmesan cheese and stir. Add chicken to Instant Pot and stir one last time to combine sauce and chicken.

11. Serve over a bed of homemade zoodles or mashed cauliflower.

CRUST-FREE PEPPERONI PIZZA

INGREDIENTS

- 1-2 Tbsp olive oil
- 1 pound Italian sausage
- 2 cups crushed tomatoes
- 1 package pepperoni
- 1/4 cup grated parmesan cheese
- 1/2 cup shredded mozzarella cheese
- 1/2 cup shredded cheddar cheese
- 1 Tbsp dried oregano
- 1/2 tsp salt
- 1/2 tsp pepper
- 1 tsp garlic powder
- 1 tsp dried basil
- 1/2 tsp onion powder
  *If you prefer less liquid, then drain tomatoes prior to adding to pot

Nutritional Information

547 total calories | 39 g fat - 351 calories | 20 g carbs - 80 calories | 29 g Protein - 116 calories

1. Set Instant Pot to sauté mode and add olive oil. When pot is "hot", add Italian sausage and cook until brown.

2. Add crushed tomatoes, oregano, salt, pepper, garlic powder, basil, and onion powder to sausage. Mix ingredients thoroughly.

3. Top tomato and sausage mixture with cheese and pepperoni (you can also try layering: tomato/sausage, cheese, and pepperoni, repeat).

4. Place lid to sealing.

5. Turn Instant Pot to manual high pressure for 7 minutes.

6. Once done cooking, do a quick release.

7. Let sit for at least 5 minutes before serving.

8. Serve with a slotted spoon (to drain any excess liquid) and top with more parmesan cheese.

FAUX MAC & CHEESE
WITH SMOKED SAUSAGE

Prep time: 10 minutes • **Cook time: 25 minutes**

INGREDIENTS

- 1 package smoked sausage
- 1-2 Tbsp olive oil
- 2 cups cauliflower rice
- 2 Tbsp cream cheese
- 1/2 cup half & half
- 1/2 cup shredded sharp cheddar cheese
- 1/8 tsp garlic powder
- 1/2 tsp salt
- 1/2 tsp ground black pepper
- Pinch of red pepper flakes (optional)

Nutritional Information

219 Total Calories | 19 g Fat - 171 Calories | 5 g Carbs - 20 Calories | 7 g Protein - 28 Calories

DIRECTIONS

1. Set Instant Pot to sauté mode on high and add olive oil. While pot is heating up, slice sausage into ¼ inch rounds and place in pot. Cook until brown on each side and then remove from pot and set aside for later.

2. In a Pyrex dish (or any other heatproof dish that will fit into pot), mix cauliflower rice, cream cheese, half & half, cheese, garlic powder, salt, and pepper. Cover with foil.

3. Pour 1 ½ cups water into Instant Pot and place trivet/steamer basket into pot. Place covered dish on trivet.

4. Set pot to manual high pressure and cook for 5 minutes. Once cooking complete, let pressure naturally release for about 10 minutes.

5. Add sausage to cauliflower mac & cheese and combine evenly (you do not need to add all sausage that was prepared, can save for later or another recipe).

6. If desired, top cooked cauliflower and sausage with additional shredded cheese and place dish under broiler. Broil until cheese is brown and begins to bubble.

7. Top with red pepper flakes, serve, and enjoy!

FIESTA CHICKEN

INGREDIENTS

- 3 lbs chicken breast, boneless, skinless
- 1/2 cup bone broth
- 4 oz cream cheese
- 1/2 cup low-sodium cottage cheese
- 1 cup salsa
- 2 tsp taco seasoning
- 1/2 avocado, diced
- 1/4 cup shredded cheddar cheese
- 1/4 cup sour cream

Nutritional Information

364 Total Calories | 20 g Fat - 180 Calories | 6 g Carbs - 24 Calories | 40 g Protein - 160 Calories

DIRECTIONS

1. Set Instant Pot to poultry setting and add chicken and broth. Cover with lid and set vent to seal. Cook for 10 minutes.

2. Once done cooking, do a quick pressure release. Make sure the internal temperature of the chicken is at least 165 degrees.

3. Remove the chicken to a large bowl. Discard some of the cooking liquid while keeping ½ cup in pot.

4. Add the cream cheese, cottage cheese, salsa, and taco seasoning to the liquid that is still in the Instant Pot.

5. Set pot to sauté mode and whisk until the cream cheese and cottage cheese have melted.

6. Shred the chicken and add back to the pot.

7. Turn setting to keep warm mode and mix all ingredients until combined.

8. Once warmed through, serve on top of cauliflower rice and top with avocado, shredded cheddar cheese, and sour cream.

GARLIC STEAMED CLAMS

Prep time: 20 minutes • **Cook time: 7 minutes**

INGREDIENTS

- 5 lb clams, alive
- 1/2 cup coconut oil or Ghee
- 1 cup white wine
- 10 cloves garlic, minced
- 2 tsp pink salt
- Fresh lemon

Nutritional Information

300 Total Calories | 24 g Fat - 216 Calories | 6 g Carbs - 24 Calories | 15 g Protein - 60 Calories

DIRECTIONS

1. Wash clams thoroughly and discard any opened ones.

2. Set Instant Pot to saute, add 1/4 cup coconut oil and garlic.

3. Saute for approx. 1 minute.

4. Pour in wine and heat for approx. 3 minutes, then add salt.

5. Add clams and cover with lid, seal vent.

6. Set pot to steam and cook for 1 minute, clams should open.

7. Remove clams from pot, and place in bowls. Leave liquid in pot.

8. Let the remaining liquid simmer by setting pot to saute, add the remaining coconut oil or ghee, and simmer for 5 mins.

9. Once done, pour liquid over clams.

NOTE: these are delicious over parmesan zoodles!

GINGER PORK SPARERIBS

INGREDIENTS

- 1 Tbsp extra virgin olive oil
- 1 Tbsp garlic, minced
- 1 Tbsp ginger, minced
- 1 1/2 lb pork spareribs, cut into pieces
- 2 Tbsp black bean garlic sauce
- 1 Tbsp rice wine
- 1 Tbsp coconut aminos
- 1/4 cup water
- 1 tsp agave nectar
- 1/3 cup scallions, chopped

Nutritional Information

418 Total Calories | 34 g Fat - 306 Calories | 6 g Carbs - 24 Calories | 22 g Protein - 88 Calories

DIRECTIONS

1. Set Instant Pot to saute mode and add oil. Once hot, add garlic and ginger. Saute 30 seconds.

2. Then add black bean garlic sauce, water, agave nectar, rice wine and coconut aminos and mix thoroughly.

3. Add pork spareribs to liquid and stir.

4. Cover Instant Pot with lid, set vent, and set to manual high pressure for 15 minutes.

5. Once done, let sit for 10 minutes and then do a quick release.

6. Serve ribs over a bed of cauliflower rice or cauliflower mash and top with chopped scallions.

HEARTY BROCCOLI AND BEEF

Prep time: 15-20 minutes • **Cook time: 10-15 minutes**

INGREDIENTS

- 2 lbs flank steak
- 3 Tbsp extra virgin olive oil
- 1 medium onion, diced
- 1 cup bone broth
- 2 Tbsp minced garlic
- 1/2 cup coconut aminos
- 2 Tbsp Stevia brown sugar
- 1 bag frozen broccoli
- 1 tsp ground ginger
- 2 Tbsp xanthum gum
- 2 Tbsp cornstarch

Nutritional Information

380 Total Calories | 20 g Fat - 180 Calories | 15 g Carbs - 60 Calories | 35 g Protein - 140 Calories

DIRECTIONS

1. Slice steak flanks (against the grain).

2. Combine coconut aminos, stevia brown sugar, ginger, broth, and garlic in a medium bowl.

3. Add steak strips to liquid mixture and let sit.

4. Turn Instant Pot to saute mode and add olive oil. Once pot is hot, add onions and saute until tender.

5. Add meat and liquid mixture to pot. Set pot to manual high pressure and cook for 10 minutes.

6. Do a quick pressure release.

7. Remove approx. 1/3 cup of liquid and add 2 Tbsp cornstarch and combine thoroughly. Add back to pot.

8. Place frozen broccoli and a cup of water in microwave and cook on high for 5 minutes

9. Drain broccoli, add to pot, mix everything together

10. Serve over cauliflower rice and enjoy

HEARTY NOODLE FREE LASAGNA

Prep time: 20 minutes or less • **Cook time: 40 minutes**

INGREDIENTS

LASAGNA

- 1-2 Tbsp olive oil
- 1 pound ground turkey
- 2 cloves minced garlic
- 1 medium onion, chopped
- 1 ½ cup ricotta cheese
- 1/2 cup grated parmesan cheese
- 1 large egg
- 3 cups of Homemade marinara sauce (see next page for recipe)
- 8-10 slices mozzarella cheese

Nutritional Information

169 Total Calories | 13 g Fat - 117 Calories | 10 g Carbs - 40 Calories | 3 g Protein - 12 Calories

DIRECTIONS

1. Set Instant Pot to sauté mode and add olive oil. Once pot is "hot", add ground turkey, garlic, and onions and cook until turkey is browned.

2. While you are waiting for the meat to brown, mix together egg, parmesan, and ricotta cheese in a small bowl.

3. Once ground turkey is browned, drain the grease from pot and add the turkey, garlic, and onion mixture to your marinara sauce made earlier, combine thoroughly.

4. For this step you will need a 1 ½ quart dish (Pyrex, Soufflé) that will fit into Instant Pot. Begin to layer the bottom of dish with ½ of the meat sauce. Top with 4 slices mozzarella cheese.

5. Layer half of ricotta cheese, parmesan, and egg mixture on top of mozzarella layer. Then top this cheese layer with the rest of the meat sauce.

6. Place 3-4 more slices of mozzarella cheese on top of meat sauce layer, then spread the remaining ricotta cheese mixture on top of this layer.

7. Use the remaining 2-3 slices of mozzarella cheese as the final layer and then cover with foil.

8. Add 1 cup water to Instant Pot and then place steamer basket/trivet in pot. Set soufflé dish on trivet and cook on manual high pressure for 8-10 minutes.

9. Once done cooking, do a quick pressure release.

10. Serve using spoon and add more cheese if desired.

HEARTY NOODLE FREE LASAGNA

INGREDIENTS

MARINARA SAUCE

- 2 Tbsp olive oil
- 2 cups chopped onion
- 1 clove minced garlic
- 2 (14.5 oz) cans diced tomatoes
- 1 ½ teaspoons dried basil
- 1 ½ teaspoons dried oregano
- 1 Tbsp salted butter
- Salt and ground black pepper to taste
- Fresh parsley

DIRECTIONS

1. Set Instant Pot to sauté. Once it reads "hot", add oil, onions, and garlic. Sauté for approx. 5 minutes.

2. Add tomatoes, oregano, and basil. Cover with lid and set to seal. Set pot to manual and cook for 10 minutes.

3. Do a quick pressure release once done cooking.

4. Next, puree the mixture. This can be done in two different ways: leave mixture in pot and use an immersion blender to puree or pour mixture into regular blender (may need to do so in small batches) and then return pureed sauce back to Instant Pot.

5. Once sauce is pureed, turn the pot to sauté mode and add butter to sauce. Cook until melted, making sure to stir. At this step you can also add salt and pepper to taste.

6. Once butter is melted add the perfect amount of salt and pepper, sprin-kle parsley and give it one last stir.

7. Remove sauce from Instant Pot and place in separate container (a sealed container if saving to make this recipe later or a large bowl so you can add sauce to lasagna tonight!). Make sure to clean Instant Pot thoroughly before moving forward to make lasagna.

JUICY BBQ SHREDDED CHICKEN WRAPS

Prep time: 10 minutes • **Cook time: 1 1/2 hours**

INGREDIENTS

- 3 lbs chicken breast
- 3 Tbsp paprika
- 1 Tbsp stevia brown sugar
- 1 Tbsp garlic powder
- 1 Tbsp dry mustard
- 3 Tbsp sea salt
- 1/4 cup apple cider vinegar
- 2 cups water
- 1/2 sweet onion, sliced
- Mayo (to taste)
- Diced avocado
- Lettuce cups
- Low-carb BBQ sauce (optional)

Nutritional Information

245 Total Calories | 9 g Fat - 81 Calories | 7 g Carbs - 28 Calories | 34 g Protein - 136 Calories

---

DIRECTIONS

1. Set Instant Pot to sauté mode and add apple cider vinegar.

2. As the vinegar is warming up, cut chicken into cubes.

3. In a medium bowl, mix paprika, **stevia** brown sugar, garlic powder, dry mustard, and sea salt together.

4. Cover all sides of cubed chicken with seasoning mixture.

5. Add chicken cubes to pot and brown each side.

6. Once browned, add water and cover with lid. Set vent to seal.

7. Set Instant Pot to manual high pressure and cook for 1 hour.

8. Once down cooking, let pressure naturally release for 10 minutes and then do a quick release for remaining pressure.

9. Shred chicken and add low-carb (keto friendly) BBQ sauce if desired.

10. Serve shredded chicken in lettuce cups with a dollop of mayo, diced avocados, and sliced sweet onions.

KETO FRIENDLY INSTANT POT CHICKEN FAJITAS

Prep time: 10-15 minutes • **Cook time: 10 minutes**

INGREDIENTS

- 2.5-3 pounds boneless, skinless chicken breast (cut into strips)
- 1 medium onion, sliced*
- 1 can (10 oz) diced tomatoes with green chiles
- 3 bell peppers (green, orange, red), sliced*
- 2 Tbsp garlic powder
- 2 Tbsp paprika
- 1 tsp chili powder
- 1 Tbsp cumin
- 1/2 tsp black pepper (can add more once meal complete if preferred)

- 2 Tbsp salt or to taste
- 3 Tbsp coconut oil
- 1-2 Tbsp fresh squeezed lime juice

Optional:
1 avocado
¼ cup shredded cheddar cheese
Lettuce cups

Nutritional Information

326 Total Calories | 18 g Fat - 162 Calories | 7 g Carbs - 28 Calories | 34 g Protein - 136 Calories

DIRECTIONS

1. Add chicken, onion, peppers, tomatoes with green chiles, seasonings, and coconut oil to instant pot and mix ingredients thoroughly.

2. Lock lid into place and set valve to seal.

3. Set instant pot to high pressure (or poultry setting) for 8 minutes. Make sure to follow the directions for your instant pot on releasing pressure from the cooker.

4. Once cooked, shred the chicken breast.

5. Add 1 Tbsp freshly squeezed lime juice (slowly add more to taste). Feel free to add extra seasonings to taste as well.

6. Mix ingredients one last time.

7. Serve in a lettuce cup and top with diced avocado and shredded cheddar cheese (as much as preferred).

*Make sure not to slice peppers or onions too thin as they may fall apart

LAMB AND CAULIFLOWER MASH

INGREDIENTS

- 4 lbs leg of lamb, boneless
- 2 Tbsp coconut oil
- 2 cups water
- 4 cloves garlic, minced

Nutritional Information

454 Total Calories | 30 g Fat - 270 Calories | 1 g Carbs - 4 Calories | 45 g Protein - 180 Calories

DIRECTIONS

1. Season lamb with salt and pepper (can use other seasonings if desired).

2. Turn Instant Pot on to saute mode and add coconut oil.

3. After heating oil for a few minutes, add the lamb to pot and brown each side.

4. Remove leg of lamb and rub minced garlic all over it.

5. Rinse out pot and add 2 cups water to pot, insert trivet, and place lamb on trivet.

6. Cover pot with lid and seal vent. Set to meat/stew mode and cook for 35-40 minutes.

7. Once done, let pressure naturally release for 10 minutes and then do a quick release.

8. When lamb is close to being done, preheat broiler.

9. Set lamb on pan and place under broiler for approx. 2 minutes.

10. Once done, let rest for 7-10 minutes before slicing.

11. Serve with cauliflower mash topped with butter and parsley.

MEXICAN MEATLOAF

Prep time: 10 minutes • **Cook time: 50 minutes**

INGREDIENTS

- 2 lbs ground grass-fed beef
- 1 cup fire roasted salsa, plus 1/4 cup divided
- 1 tsp cumin
- 1 tsp garlic powder
- 1 tsp chili powder
- 1 tsp paprika
- 1 tsp onion powder
- 1 tsp sea salt (or more to taste)
- 1 tsp ground black pepper
- 1 large yellow onion, diced
- 1 large egg
- 1/4 cup xanthan gum
- 1 Tbsp avocado oil

Nutritional Information

354 Total Calories | 22 g Fat - 198 Calories | 9 g Carbs - 36 Calories | 30 g Protein - 120 Calories

DIRECTIONS

1. Pour 1 cup water into Instant Pot.

2. Combine all ingredients in a bowl, mixing together well by hand (reserving 1/4 cup of the salsa).

3. Form a loaf with your meat mixture, pressing it together firmly.

4. Spoon the 1/4 cup of remaining fire roasted salsa on top of your meatloaf.

5. Wrap it tightly in foil.

6. Insert trivet into pot and place the foil wrapped meatloaf on trivet.

7. Close the lid, seal vent, select the Pressure Cook/Manual button.

8. Adjust the time until 35 minutes is displayed.

9. Do a quick pressure release.

10. Remove your meatloaf.

11. Serve with fresh cilantro sprigs.

SAUSAGE AND GREEN BEANS

Prep time: 3 minutes • **Cook time: 10 minutes**

INGREDIENTS

- 2 cups low-sodium chicken broth
- 2 16 oz. frozen green beans
- 16 oz. chicken sausage, sliced
- 1/2 yellow onion, diced
- 2 tsp seasoning salt

Nutritional Information

310 Total Calories | 22 g Fat - 198 Calories | 7 g Carbs - 28 Calories | 21 g Protein - 84 Calories

1. Place all ingredients in the Instant Pot.

2. Cover with lid on and make sure the vent is closed.

3. Set pot to manual high pressure and cook for 6 minutes.

4. When done, do a quick pressure release.

5. Serve with cheesy cauliflower mac and cheese.

SMOTHERED MUSHROOM PORK CHOPS

Prep time: 10 minutes • **Cook time: 30 minutes**

INGREDIENTS

- 4 (6 ounce) boneless pork loin chops
- 1 Tbsp paprika
- 1 tsp garlic powder
- 1 tsp onion powder
- 1 tsp salt
- 1 tsp ground black pepper
- 2 Tbsp coconut oil
- 1 cup yellow onion, sliced
- 8 oz baby bella mushrooms, sliced
- 1 Tbsp butter
- 1/2 cup heavy whipping cream
- 1/8 – 1/4 teaspoon guar gum
  (can also use xanthan gum)

Nutritional Information

269 Total Calories | 17 g Fat - 153 Calories | 5 g Carbs - 20 Calories | 24 g Protein - 96 Calories

DIRECTIONS

1. Turn Instant Pot to sauté setting and add coconut oil. While pot is heating up, mix together paprika, ground black pepper, garlic powder, salt, onion powder.

2. Portion out 1 Tbsp of mixed seasonings and rub on top and bottom of pork chop. Set the remaining spices aside for later.

3. Once pot is "hot", brown the pork chops on each side (approx. 3 mins per side).

4. Once browned, turn off Instant Pot and remove pork chops. Place the sliced onions and mushrooms in the pot and then place the browned chops on top. Cover with lid and set the vent to seal.

5. Cook on manual high for 25 minutes (internal temp of pork chops should be at least 145 degrees. If you check and it is lower, cook on high for additional 1 min).

6. After pork chops are fully cooked, do either a natural or quick pressure release. Turn off pot.

7. Remove only the pork chops and place on plate, cover with foil to keep warm.

8. Set the Instant Pot to sauté mode again and add the remaining seasonings, butter, and heavy cream. Whisk ingredients together. Add 1/8 tsp guar gum and whisk again.

9. Let this simmer until butter melts & sauce starts to thicken (approx. 3-5 minutes).

10. Turn off pot. If the sauce is not thickened enough to your preference, then gradually add more guar gum (1/8 teaspoon at a time). Keep in mind that the sauce will continue to thicken as it cools.

11. Remove foil from pork chops and top with mushroom and onion gravy and enjoy!

SPICED-UP CHEESE FRITTATA

Prep time: 10 minutes • **Cook time: 30 minutes**

INGREDIENTS

- 4 eggs
- 1 cup half & half
- 10 oz can diced green chiles
- 1/2 tsp ground cumin
- 1/2 tsp chili powder
- 1/2 tsp salt
- 1/2 tsp ground black pepper
- 1/2 cup shredded cheddar cheese*
- 1/2 cup shredded mozzarella cheese*
- 1/4 cup sour cream
- 1 avocado
  *Divide cheese in half (1/4 cup each)
   and set aside for later

Nutritional Information

338 Total Calories | 26 g Fat - 234 Calories | 11 g Carbs - 44 Calories | 15 g Protein - 60 Calories

1. Grease a 6-inch metal pan with 1-2 tbsp olive oil (or butter).

   *Make sure that pan is covered thoroughly.

2. In a medium bowl, whisk eggs, half & half, green chiles, cumin, chili powder, salt,

   pepper, ¼ cup cheddar cheese, and ¼ cup mozzarella cheese.

3. Pour egg mixture into greased pan and cover with foil.

4. Add 2 cups water to Instant Pot and place steamer basket/trivet in pot.

5. Place covered pan onto steamer basket/trivet.

6. Cook on high pressure for 20 minutes. Once complete, allow pressure to naturally

   release for approximately 10 minutes and then do quick release.

7. Carefully remove pan from instant pot and take off foil.

8. Sprinkle the remaining cheese on top of frittata and place under broiler for 5 minutes

   or until cheese begins to bubble.

9. Remove from broiler and serve with a side of sour cream and diced avocado.

SPICY QUESO CHICKEN

Prep time: 15 minutes • **Cook time: 30 minutes**

INGREDIENTS

- 2 large boneless skinless chicken breast halves
- 2 Tbsp taco seasoning
- 1/2 tsp chipotle powder
- 2, 14.5 oz cans diced tomatoes with green chiles, do not drain
- 1/4 tsp salt
- 2 cups low-sodium chicken broth
- 1 cup green salsa
- 8 oz cream cheese, softened
- 1 ripe avocado, diced
- 1 cup cheddar cheese for topping

Nutritional Information

490 Total Calories | 33 g Fat - 297 Calories | 22 g Carbs - 88 Calories | 20 g Protein - 80 Calories

1. Place chicken, taco seasoning, chipotle powder, tomatoes with green chiles, salt, broth and green salsa in Instant Pot.

2. Set to manual high pressure and cook for 10 minutes.

3. Allow pressure to release naturally (about 15 minutes), remove chicken and shred (leave liquid in pot). Set chicken aside.

4. Stir softened cream cheese into liquid left in the pot and whisk until fully melted.

5. Return chicken to the soup and serve with diced avocado and cheese on top.

SWEET AND SPICY SALMON

Prep time: 5-10 minutes • **Cook time: 10 minutes**

INGREDIENTS

- 2 5 oz salmon filets
- 1 cup water

Sauce ingredients:
- 2 cloves garlic, minced
- Lime juice from 1 freshly squeezed lime
- 1 jalapeño, diced and seeded
- 1 Tbsp sugar-free honey
- 1 Tbsp hot water

Sauce ingredients:
- 1 Tbsp avocado oil
- 1/2 tsp paprika
- 1/2 tsp cumin
- chopped scallions (topping)

Nutritional Information

351 Total Calories | 19 g Fat - 171 Calories | 9 g Carbs - 36 Calories | 36 g Protein - 144 Calories

DIRECTIONS

1. Make the sauce first by adding all sauce ingredients into a bowl and whisk until combined. Set aside.

2. Pour 1 cup water into pot and insert steamer basket. Place salmon on top and cover pot with lid.

3. Seal vent and set Instant Pot to steam mode on high, cook for 5 minutes.

4. Once done, do a quick release and serve salmon on plate.

5. Pour sauce over salmon and top with scallions.

6. Enjoy as is or serve with cauliflower mash and butter.

ZUCCHINI LAYERED LASAGNA

Prep time: 20 minutes • **Cook time: 1 hour**

INGREDIENTS

- 1 Large zucchini, thinly sliced
- 2 lbs ground beef
- 1 medium yellow onion, diced
- 1 14 oz can diced tomatoes
- 1 cup fresh basil, chopped finely
- 8 cloves garlic, minced
- 2 Tbsp coconut oil
- 1 cup low-sodium cottage cheese
- 1 cup mozzarella cheese, shredded
- 1 cup cheddar cheese, shredded

Nutritional Information

486 Total Calories | 30 g Fat - 270 Calories | 9 g Carbs - 36 Calories | 45 g Protein - 180 Calories

DIRECTIONS

1. Set Instant Pot to saute mode and add 2 Tbsp coconut oil, onion, garlic, and beef.

2. Saute until onions are tender and meat is browned

3. Add diced tomatoes (with the liquid) and simmer for 30 minutes, stirring occassionally.

4. After 30 minutes, remove meat sauce and rinse pot.

5. Layer a thin portion of meat sauce on bottom of dish, top with a layer of zucchini,

6. Then a layer of cottage cheese. Do this 3 times.

7. Once done layering, add mozzarella cheese on top.

8. Use a heatproof dish that fits into Instant Pot for #6-7.

9. Cover dish with foil

10. Add 1 cup water to pot, insert trivet, and place dish on trivet

11. Place lid on pot, seal vent, cook 20 mins on manual high pressure.

DESSERTS

VANILLA COCONUT CUSTARD

INGREDIENTS

- 1 cup unsweetened coconut milk
- 3 eggs
- 1 cup Swerve or similar sweetener
- 1/8-1/4 tsp vanilla extract

Nutritional Information

261 Total Calories | 19 g Fat - 171 Calories | 2 g Carbs - 8 Calories | 19 g Protein - 76 Calories

1. Blend eggs, Swerve, vanilla extract, and milk together.

2. Pour mixture into Pyrex dish that fits into Instant Pot.

3. Cover with foil.

4. Pour 2 cups of water into pot, place trivet in pot, and place dish onto trivet.

5. Turn Instant Pot to manual high pressure and cook for 30 minutes.

6. Once done, naturally release pressure for 10 mins and then quick release remaining pressure.

7. Test consistency with a knife by placing it in center of custard. If it comes out clean, then it is done.

8. Cool in fridge until custard is set.

CHOCOLATE COCONUT MOUSSE

Prep time: 10 minutes • **Cook time: 15-20 minutes**

INGREDIENTS

- 4 egg yolks
- 3/8 tsp Stevia extract
  (or can use ½ cup Monkfruit)
- 1/4 cup water
- 1/4 cup cacao
- 1 cup heavy whipping cream
- 1/2 cup coconut milk
- 1/2 tsp vanilla
- ¼- ½ tsp sea salt

Nutritional Information

293 total calories | 29 g fat - 261 calories | 4 g carbs - 16 calories | 4 g Protein - 16 calories

DIRECTIONS

Needs to cool for 4 hours in the refrigerator before eating.

1. Whisk egg yolks in a bowl until beaten thoroughly.

2. Combine Stevia extract, cacao, and water in a sauce pan and warm on low heat until cacao is combined and Stevia is melted (be careful not to burn liquid).

3. Add coconut milk and whipping cream to pan and continue to whisk. Do not bring liquid to a boil, but let mixture heat up and then turn off burner and remove pan from stove. Mix in salt and vanilla.

4. Let the liquid cool slightly (so you don't begin to cook the eggs) and add approx. 1 Tbsp of liquid into your egg yolks, whisk briefly. Continue whisking as you gradually pour the remainder of the chocolate and milk mixture into the egg yolks.

5. Once evenly combined, pour into mason jars or ramekins (distribute evenly).

6. Pour 1 ½ cup water to Instant Pot and place trivet/steamer basket in pot. Place jars or ramekins on trivet and cover with foil.

7. Cover pot with lid and set vent to seal.

8. Set pot to manual pressure and cook for 6 minutes, then do a quick release once down cooking.

9. Remove jars CAREFULLY.

10. Let them cool fully before placing them in the refrigerator for at least 4 hours (they are best served cold).

CHOCOLATE PEANUT BUTTER CAKE

Prep time: 5 minutes • **Cook time: 12 minutes**

INGREDIENTS

- 2 large eggs
- 2 Tbsp stevia
- 1/2 tsp baking powder
- 2 Tbsp heavy cream
- 1 tsp vanilla extract
- 1/4 cup baking cocoa
- 2 Tbsp peanut butter
- 1 Tbsp Hershey's sugar-free chocolate syrup

Nutritional Information

271 total calories | 19 g fat - 171 calories | 13 g carbs - 52 calories | 12 g Protein - 48 calories

1. Spray 2 ramekins with cooking spray and set aside.

2. In a medium bowl, mix together stevia, baking powder, and cocoa.

3. Once combined, add eggs, heavy cream and vanilla extract. Whisk until smooth.

4. Fill ramekins about halfway with cake mixture.

5. Add 1 cup water to Instant Pot.

6. Place steamer basket/trivet in pot and place ramekins on top.

7. Place lid to close and set vent to seal.

8. Turn on to manual high pressure and cook for 9 minutes.

9. Do a quick release and remove ramekins.

10. Flip over ramekins on to plate in order to release the cake from the cups.

11. Add peanut butter and chocolate syrup on top of cake and enjoy!

COCOA AND PEANUT CHEESECAKE

Prep time: 10 minutes • **Cook time: 20 minutes**

INGREDIENTS

- 16 oz cream cheese
- 2 eggs
- 2 Tbsp powdered peanut butter
- 1 Tbsp cocoa
- 1 tsp vanilla extract
- 3 tsp liquid stevia
- 1/2 cup crushed peanuts
- 1/4 cup whipped cream

Nutritional Information

382 total calories | 34 g fat - 306 calories | 8 g carbs - 32 calories | 11 g Protein - 44 calories

DIRECTIONS

1. Blend cream cheese and eggs in a blender until smooth.

2. Add remaining ingredients, except peanuts, and blend.

3. Once everything is blended until smooth, distribute evenly into 8 ounce mason jars and cover with foil.

4. Pour 1 cup of water in Instant Pot, place trivet into pot, and then place jars on trivet.

5. Turn Instant Pot to manual high pressure, cook for 15 minutes.

6. Release pressure naturally for 10 minutes, then quick release.

7. Refrigerate for at least 4 hours (or overnight).

8. Once ready, top with peanuts and whipped cream.

SPICED CARROT CAKE

INGREDIENTS

- 3 eggs
- 1 cup almond flour
- 4 tsp liquid Stevia
- 1/2 tsp cinnamon
- 1/8 tsp ground nutmeg
- 1/8 tsp ground allspice
- 1/4 cup coconut oil
- 1/2 cup heavy whipping cream
- 1 cup carrots, shredded
- 1/2 cup walnuts, chopped
- 1 tsp baking powder

Nutritional Information

336 Total Calories | 32 g Fat - 288 Calories | 5 g Carbs - 20 Calories | 7 g Protein - 28 Calories

DIRECTIONS

1. Find a cake pan that will fit into Instant Pot (approx. 6").

2. Grease pan.

3. Add ingredients into a bowl and mix with hand mixer until thoroughly combined.

4. Pour mixture into the cake pan and cover with foil.

5. Pour 2 cups water into pot, insert trivet/steamer basket into pot, and place pan onto trivet.

6. Set Instant Pot to Cake mode and cook for 40 mins or cook on manual high pressure for 30 mins.

7. Once done, release pressure naturally for 10 mins.

8. Allow to cool, then serve and enjoy!

23044363R00076

Made in the USA
Columbia, SC
02 August 2018